BEHIND the SCENES of a MUSICAL

Silver Books
Series Editor: Julia Eccleshare

Rhymoceros Leo Aylen
Why the Agouti Has No Tail Floella Benjamin
The Computer Nut Betsy Byars
Not Many People Know That! Michael Caine
Real Life Monsters Richard Davis
Endangered Species Richard Davis
The Siege of Babylon Farrukh Dhondy
Two into One Won't Go Terry Deary
Grow Your Own Poems Peter Dixon
Everest Without Oxygen Tony Feldman
Is That It? Bob Geldof
Voyage Adèle Geras
Electric Heroes Mick Gowar
Refugees, Evacuees Charles Hannam
Chips and Jessie Shirley Hughes
Boo to a Goose John Mole
News From The Front Nicholas Nugent
How a Film is Made Bruce Purchase
Behind the Scenes of a Musical Bruce Purchase
Journey of 1000 Miles Ian Strachan
Toothache and Tremors Guy Williams
Magic Guy Williams
There's a Wolf in my Pudding David Henry Wilson

BEHIND the SCENES of a MUSICAL

Bruce Purchase

For Meg, Alex and Kate

© Bruce Purchase 1990

All rights reserved. No reproduction, copy or transmission of this publication may be made without written permission

No paragraph of this publication may be reproduced, copied or transmitted save with written permission or in accordance with the provisions of the Copyright Act 1956 (as amended), or under the terms of any licence permitting limited copying issued by the Copyright Licensing Agency, 33–4 Alfred Place, London WC1E 7DP

Any person who does any unauthorised act in relation to this publication may be liable to criminal prosecution and civil claims for damages.

First published 1990

Published by
MACMILLAN EDUCATION LTD
Houndsmills, Basingstoke, Hampshire RG21 2XS
and London
Companies and representatives
throughout the world

Series design Julian Holland
Cover photograph by the author

Printed in Hong Kong

British Library Cataloguing in Publication Data
Purchase, Bruce
Behind the scenes of a musical.
1. Children's musical shows. Production – Manuals
I. Title
782.81′07
ISBN 0-333-48919-5

CONTENTS

A note on the author 6
Cast list 7

Curtain up 9
Birth of an idea 11
The script 13
Choosing the children 17
Actors – getting the job 20
The children visit the theatre 22
The actors meet 24
Rehearsals at school 27
Actors in rehearsal 29
The children's costumes 32
Actors' costumes and make-up 35
Joint rehearsal 37
First night 42
The actors in performance 45
The children in performance 48
After the show 50

A note on the author

Bruce Purchase was born in New Zealand and came to the UK on a New Zealand government bursary to study acting at RADA.

He was a founder acting member of the National Theatre, under the direction of Laurence Olivier, and has also been for several years a member of the Royal Shakespeare Company, Nottingham Playhouse and the Bristol Old Vic. He played the title role of Othello to Bernard Miles' Iago at the Mermaid Theatre.

His film credits include *Mary, Queen of Scots* and *Macbeth*; and he has worked for many years in television, including such series as *I, Claudius*, *Dr Who*, *Clayhanger*, and as Squire Trelawney in *Return to Treasure Island*.

The photographs in this book are all the author's own, and thus convey a true 'actor's eye-view' of the theatre.

Acknowledgements

I would like to thank Brenda Stones, whose advice on the structure and sequence of this book was invaluable; also thanks to my friends from *The Pied Piper*, including the children who played the rats.

Thanks are also due to Adrian Mitchell and to Oberon Books for reproduction of text from the script of *The Pied Piper* as well as comments from the teachers and children who took part.

The children appearing in *The Pied Piper* were from the following ILEA primary schools: Addison, Bonner, Bridishe, Canonbury, Childeric, Christ Church, Columbia, Colville, Deptford Park, Dog Kennel Hill, Drayton Park, Dulwich Hamlet, Gayhurst, Grasmere, Grinling Gibbons, Hollydale, Kenmont, Lauriston, Lucas Vale, New End, St. Francis, St. John's and St. Clement's, Sir Thomas Abney, Stebon and Streatham Wells, and from the KIDS UK Theatre Group.

Cast list

The Pied Piper   Sylvester McCoy
Toffee Jenkins   Diane Bull
Baron Dennis Saveloy   Philip McGough
Lady Lucy Saveloy   Patsy Rowlands
The Honourable Egbert Saveloy   Bill Moody
King Rat   Brian Hibbard
Nutter Mausenheimer   Bruce Purchase
Cosima Beamer   Doreen Webster
Doctor Thelonius Mungadory   Allister Bain
Arianalla Skiller   Mary Askham
Boggle   Ewart James Walters
Goggle   Jimmy Chisholm
Children of Hamelin   the children
Lamplighters   Bruce Purchase, Allister Bain
The Rodents   Mary Askham, Doreen Webster
The Massed Rats   the children
The Rampant Umbrage   Brian Hibbard
The Iced Knight   Mary Askham

Backstage

Director   Alan Cohen
Script   Adrian Mitchell
Music   Dominic Muldowney
Settings   Roger Glossop
Costumes   Sally Gardner
Movement   David Toguri
Lighting   Paul McLeish
Sound   Paul Groothuis with Paul Arditti
Stage manager   Liz Markham
Musical director   Robert Lockhart
Staff director   Sarah Ream

Hamelin Herald

NEW IMPROVED

CITIZENS IN PROTEST
see page 2

TODAY
THEATRE COMPANY STAGES NEW VERSION OF PIED PIPER
Turn to page 4.

RATS! RATS! RATS!

CITY UNDER SIEGE
by ROBERT 'GRAVY' BROWNING

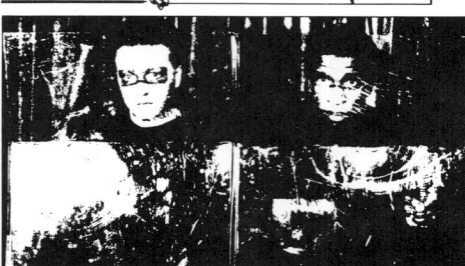

A plague of rats, that is what this city is suffering from. Every day the crisis gets worse, and all the City Council does is make excuses.

Rampaging
Yesterday some determined Hameliners took matters into their own hands and formed a Citizens Action Group. The mayor, Baron Saveloy, was accused of being "a noddy" and warned that if nothing was done about the rats soon "we'll send you packing". A further meeting is planned for today.

Meanwhile rampaging rats are attacking children, cats and dogs, and eating huge amounts of food, including grain, flour, fish, and cheese. Even worse,

the creatures spoil several times as much food as they eat.

Resigned
The city faces this catastrophe without an official rat catcher. Mr. Stephen Sanderson, 46, the Municipal Rat Catcher for the last 18½ years, resigned yesterday. "I suppose things have got a bit out of control," he admitted. "I never wanted to be a rat catcher anyway. I trained as an ice-cream salesman."

Waffle
At a press conference last night, Mayor Saveloy agreed that the rats were "a headache" but advised people not to panic. "We'll sort things out at our banquet" he promised.

Editorial Comment page 2

Baron Dennis Saveloy

The Mayor's security guards, Boggle and Goggle (pictured above), walked free from court yesterday. Judge Ronnie Saveloy (the Mayor's cousin) ordered the jury to bring in verdicts of 'not guilty' on 26 charges of assault and mayhem. "These men are fine, upstanding guardians of law and order", said the judge. "Just because the heads and noses of a few hooligans came into accidental contact with their truncheons, is no reason to make a fuss."

STOP PRESS Guided Tours of Hamelin Sewers have been indefinitely suspended due to rodent infestation.

The Hamelin Herald, produced by the National Theatre as a programme

The expectant audience

Curtain up

As the house lights dim, the buzz of conversation in the audience softens to almost total silence. The darkened rows of children and adults are quiet with expectation.

The Piper, Toffee and Egbert make their entrances

The audience can detect the figures of the principal actors and the smaller figures of the children in costume crossing the stage as shadows, to take up their first positions.

After a moment, the silence and the darkness are broken abruptly by an eruption of sound and light. The audience all join in shouts of support, and the whole cast bursts into the first song:

> *Hamelin Town's in Brunswick*
> *By famous Hanover City;*
> *The river Weser, deep and wide,*
> *Washes its walls on the southern side . . .*

The curtain is up on *The Pied Piper*, the National Theatre's production of a children's musical, with a cast of local children playing the parts of rats and children.

A group of rats

The children dancing

Birth of an idea

How did all this come about? Why did the National Theatre decide to add to its normal cast of actors by giving hundreds of local children the chance to dress up as rats and join a professional production?

We can trace the story back. The theatre directors knew that they wanted to put on a children's musical for Christmas, but they weren't sure which one to choose or how to make it different.

The director, Alan Cohen, with one of the professional cast

11

Alan Cohen, a resident associate director, finally came up with the idea of *The Pied Piper*, adapting the original long poem by Robert Browning. Kevin Cahill of the theatre's Education Department liked the idea, and the final go-ahead was given by the Artistic Director, Sir Peter Hall.

They then approached the writer and poet Adrian Mitchell, to ask him to write the script and lyrics. Adrian was keen to try, so at last the project was underway.

> *But when begins our ditty*
> *Almost five hundred years ago,*
> *To see the townsfolk suffer so*
> *From vermin, was a pity . . .*

The director with his lead actor, Sylvester McCoy, off duty

The idea of the rats in Hamelin invading the town is central to the poem. But the problem was that to employ enough young professional actors for these crowd scenes would be very costly. What could be the solution?

'Let's bring children out of the audience to join in the show.'

'Too difficult. It could be chaotic.'

Kevin at last came up with a brilliant idea. They should contact the Inner London Education Authority and ask if schools would let local children join the show, to play two kinds of part: the rats and also the children of Hamelin.

ILEA asked their teachers what they thought, and the response was enthusiastic. They would love their pupils to have the opportunity to join in.

One problem was how you bring together the different patterns of life of theatre and schools: the theatre works late into the night, whereas schools, of course, operate during the day, in set periods. But parents were perfectly happy for the children to work outside schools hours, so the idea went ahead.

The script

Meanwhile the scriptwriter, Adrian Mitchell, was hard at work on the text and lyrics.

He decided to make various changes to the folk story, so that it would work better on the stage.

The Pied Piper with the Mayor of Hamelin's son, the Honourable Egbert Saveloy

The central character was, of course, the Pied Piper, to be played by Sylvester McCoy. This actor was already well-known from TV shows like *'Tiswas'*, *'Eureka'*, *'Dramarama'* and especially *'Dr Who'*.

In the original poem there was a crippled boy, who played a poignant role in being left behind outside the mountain. Instead, Adrian Mitchell decided to create a part for a crippled girl, Toffee Jenkins, because there were so few other parts for girls.

He then built up the role of the Mayor of Hamelin, and made him a bumptious character who resisted change in his city. All the members of the Mayor's family, the Saveloys, became figures of fun in the play.

Finally, the scriptwriter created parts for two Darth Vader-type characters: Boggle and Goggle, Dr Mungadory, and trades people from the city who ran the sweet stall, the toy stall and the bakery.

The plot of the musical version followed much the same story-line as the original poem: Hamelin was a peaceful town in Germany, enjoying its trade and family life, until it was invaded by a pestilential plague of rats. They descended by night, and ate the food from the table and terrorised the children of the town.

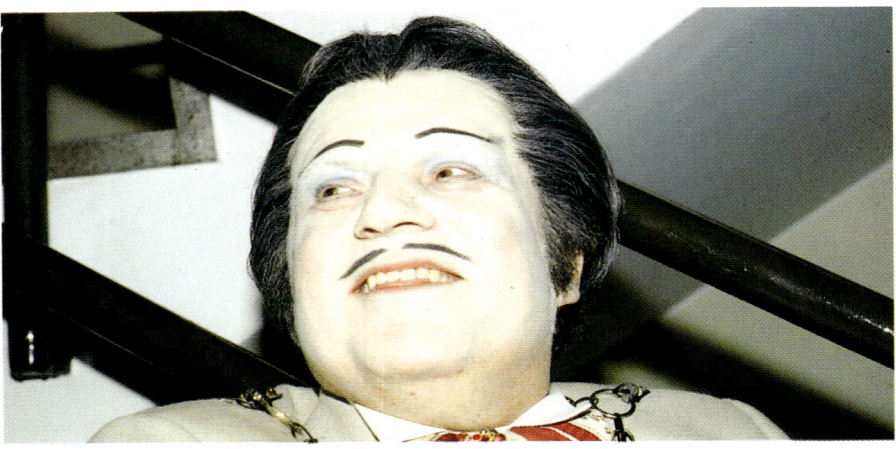

The Mayor himself, Baron Dennis Saveloy

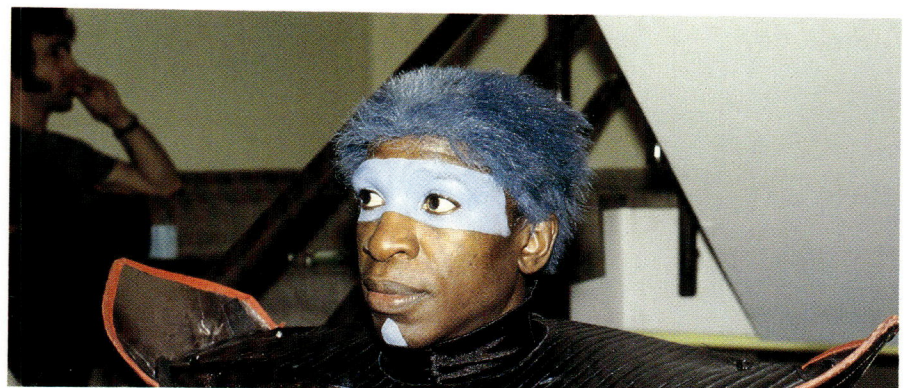

One of the two security guards, Boggle and Goggle

Dr Thelonius Mungadory, a learned seller of potions

15

One day the Pied Piper arrived in Hamelin and offered to rid the town of its rats. The mayor was delighted and promised him a thousand crowns to do the job. So at dead of night the piper drew out his magic pipe and charmed the rats out of the sewers and cellars. He led them down to the river, where they all dived from the banks and were drowned.

But the Mayor was such an untrustworthy character that he refused to pay the reward. The piper was furious, and to get his revenge he decided to lure the children of the city out of their homes and take them to the magic mountain.

The monster, the Rampant Umbrage, played by Brian Hibbard of the Flying Pickets

Here there were plenty of opportunities to turn the children's journey into a magical quest: over the Shivering Bridge of Dilvergibbon, through the Bottomless Swamp of Ombroglio, into the Freezing Forest of Forafter and on to the mystic Koppelburg Mountain.

They met strange characters all along the way: the Rampant Umbrage, the Iced Knight, but just managed to survive the journey. Only Toffee Jenkins limped behind, and she was left outside the mountain as a shooting star flashed overhead, and the children of Hamelin were lost forever.

Choosing the children

So the first part of the show needed rats – crowds of them, herds of them, troops of them. The children loved this part best – dressing in sinister black, dancing their rat dances and singing their rat songs.

A rat's mask

The childrens' cloaks

Girls from the show

The contrast was the second half, when they turned into innocent children, but still with fabulous costumes and raucous songs.

Of course, children are cheaper to use than professional actors; but the main advantage of inviting children to share the performance was the opportunity for them to see at first hand how a professional theatre operates. It also helped to bridge the gap between professional performers and the children in the audience.

The National Theatre started by approaching local schools for children's parts, in Lewisham, Hackney and Tower Hamlets. Each time a cast of about fifty was selected, so that by the end of the six month season a total of 850 children had a chance to join in!

Toffee Jenkins out in school with the children

A school party arrives to see the show

What it meant for the children was some extra work outside school hours; time spent in school and at the theatre, practising routines and making costumes; rehearsal and repetition – but a fabulous experience of real-life grease paint.

Actors – getting the job

So how do I know all this? What was my role in the production?

I am a professional actor, and my previous jobs have all been in film, TV and adult theatre, so that I knew almost nothing about the world of children's musicals. I was therefore totally surprised when the phone rang and my agent Joyce was on the line, to say I'd been invited to try for the part of the Miller. The miller's name was Nutter Mausenheimer. 'Nutter' was to be my name!

The part demanded a tall person (which I am), with a fat stomach (which I didn't have, but that kind of thing can be arranged with padding!). And I was to skip around the stage in a cloud of flour, clapping my hands together and setting off powdery explosions wherever I trod.

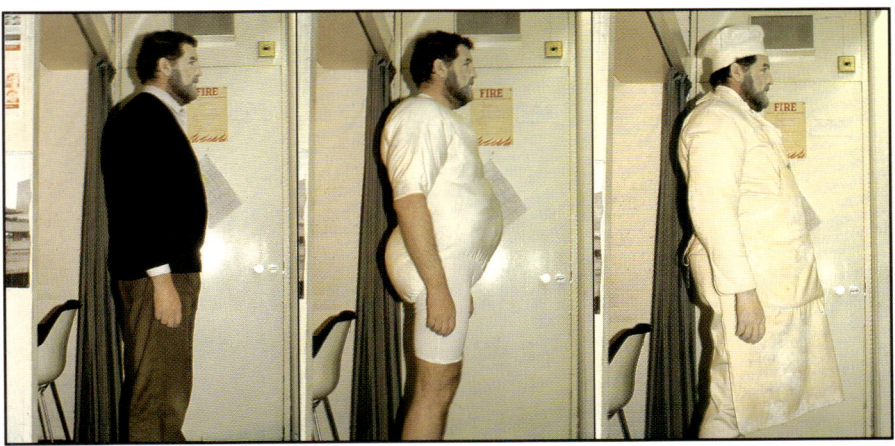

Myself, normal shape

Padding to create the fat stomach and bottom!

The fully dressed miller

Painting a miller's face

The miller gets a hair-cut

What did I have to do to get the part? Sing a song (which I hadn't done for years), dance a jig (which I hadn't done for even more years) and talk to the director and the composer about the show and how they saw my role.

I was even more surprised when my agent rang a second time – I had the part!

The children visit the theatre

Once we'd all been selected, principal actors and school children, it was time to introduce us all to the theatre.

The rats came in one day – all 850 of them. A real plague of rats descending on the National Theatre!

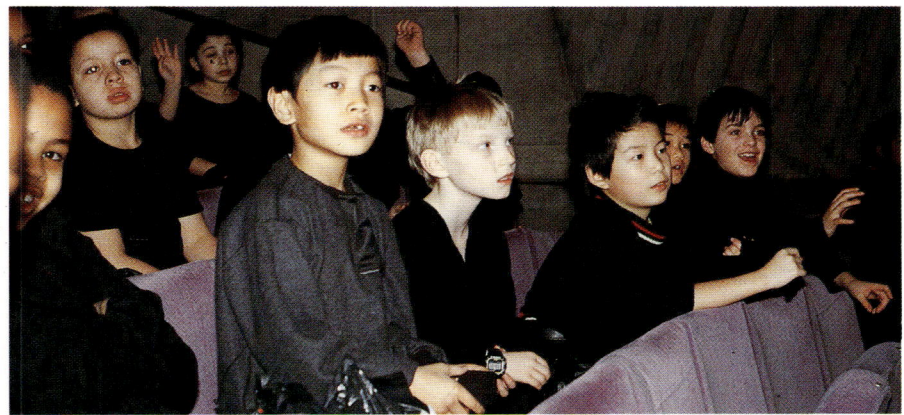

The purpose of that day was to leave the children to clamber up on the stage and have a good look around, hear about the story, meet everyone involved and ask questions, so that they became familiar with their surroundings. We called it RAT DAY! Most of the 850 had never been in a theatre – certainly not one as big as the Olivier auditorium, which is huge, seating 1400 people.

One child turned to me and said – 'The ceiling's as high as a tower block!'

The children arriving at the theatre to rehearse

Rats trying out their masks

Sylvester McCoy and Jimmy Chisholm (Goggle) meeting the team

The actors meet

We had our first day, too. On that day the principal actors gathered together in a large, barn-like hall in Islington to read the play together for the first time, and afterwards to talk together with everyone involved about the aims of the production.

Ewart James Walters (Boggle)

24

Allister Bain (Dr Mungadory) at rehearsal in the theatre

Roger Glossop, who designed the set, showed us a beautifully intricate model of what the final stage would look like. He described in great detail how it would all work – how the miller's wheel would move, how mechanical rats (instead of cuckoos!) would pop out of clocks, how the trucks would be moved by stage technicians to transform the town of Hamelin into the Freezing Forest of Forafter, with snow falling from above. Then he showed us how the mountain would be created, within seconds, from a huge sheet of gauze. With clever use of light, the audience would be able to view into the very heart of the mountain, where the children would be happily dancing and singing. The effects were all stunning.

Sally Gardner, the costume designer, then showed us individual drawings for all the costumes. She had chosen bright, vivid colours and exaggerated shapes, which were just right for the young audience who would be coming to this show.

Alan Cohen, the director, described the approach he would take in the production and what the pattern of the early days of rehearsal would entail.

Adrian Mitchell explained how he'd arrived at his final working script, and described his vision of all the characters in the play.

Adrian had written the text of the songs for the show, but the music was all composed by Dominic Muldowney. Since the impact of the music was to be so important in *The Pied Piper*, Dominic was a vital member of the team.

David Toguri, the choreographer, was the one who put us through our dance steps, and he instructed us to bring tracksuits to wear for our physical workouts before rehearsal each day. I groaned at the thought of all the physical exercise we were in for.

'Do you really think you'll get *me* to dance, David?' I said, and he grinned back: 'I'll get you high-kicking before I've finished with you!'

Egbert and Toffee Jenkins in rehearsal

Liz Markham, the stage manager, and her team indicated where the call sheets would be posted, where rehearsal props would be laid out, and how the myriad of coloured tapes stuck to the floor of the rehearsal area related to the design of the set. Then she went on to the vital question of how to pay for our tea and coffee, and answered questions on the thousand and one other details that stage managers are responsible for during rehearsal. Finally, representatives from the make-up, wigs and wardrobe departments came in to take our measurements and check our appearances.

Any nervousness we might have felt soon evaporated with all the activity. I could tell they would be a good team to work with.

Rehearsals at school

Meanwhile, the children were getting stuck into their rehearsals at school.

They were trained, not by their own teachers, but by the special teachers employed by the theatre, who visited the schools for special sessions.

Diane Bull, who played Toffee Jenkins, also went into school to help with rehearsals

Robina Nicolson was in charge of teaching the songs and Jennie Buckman was responsible for all the dance, movement and mime. Each school, depending on their experience, needed a minimum of six visits from Jennie and another six from Robina.

A strict timetable had to be worked out to get everything done on time. In between Jennie and Robina's official visits, teachers within each school found time in their busy schedules to keep the work going so that the children didn't go 'off the boil'. Steady progress was made. Some teachers attended workshops in the theatre to find out exactly what was required of their pupils.

Hetty Shand, from the theatre's Education Department, provided crucial planning. Every three weeks she issued a detailed planning schedule to each of the schools involved at that stage – covering a total of thirteen schools over a six month period.

When Jennie and Robina first met each group of children, they started by assessing the capabilities of each group through movement and singing exercises, deciding how much time would be needed in the preparation of each group. Rehearsals began in earnest six weeks before each group's first performance.

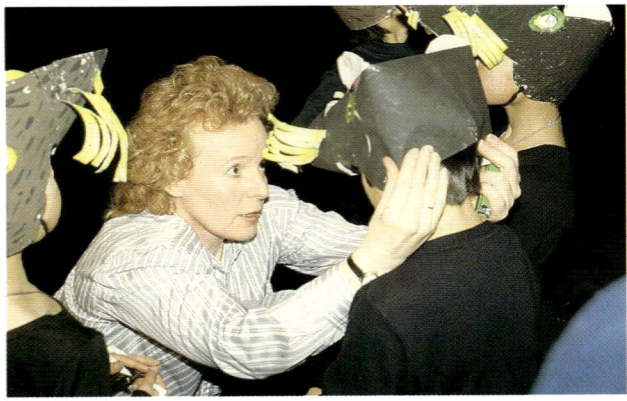

Robina getting the children ready for music practice

You can imagine the organisation! Several schools at any one time were at different stages of development within the rehearsal process. One teacher expressed it well when she said, 'Although it was an exciting time for us all, it did involve a lot of weeping and gnashing of teeth to prepare the children in time for their first appearance.'

Most of the children had never been in a theatre before, and certainly none had performed on so huge a stage. But to some the experience was even stranger: they were newly arrived in the UK, with English as their second language, and therefore knew very few words of English at all. I remember one Turkish boy, his face a study in amazement as he sang, in this new foreign language, the songs he'd just been taught by heart, for he'd only been in the country a matter of weeks!

The children loved working on the show with us just as much as we did with them. It became in the best sense like a continuing party, thanks to the valuable preparation put in by Jennie, Robina and all the teachers.

Actors in rehearsal

On the professional stage, our rehearsals started in earnest the day after the read-through.

Each day started with a physical warm-up under the direction of David Toguri, the choreographer. We usually began with a slow jog round the rehearsal room, increasing in speed to a fast run. Then followed a variety of stretching exercises and competitive team games, when we'd be divided into groups to compete in some fast and difficult race. After half an hour we'd be thoroughly warmed-up and ready to rehearse. By then we were all bathed in sweat, with muscles screaming! However, during the rehearsal period I became very fit – well prepared for the rigours of the six month season that lay ahead! During these work-outs, David often gave us basic dance sequences to practise. He, like Jennie and Robina in the schools, was assessing us, both individually and as a group, to find our strengths and weaknesses.

The rest of the day would include placing (or blocking) the moves of the production, and then David began to suggest dance sequences for the songs.

King Rat waiting to rehearse (Brian Hibbard again)

Robert Lockhart, the musical director, at the keyboard for music rehearsals

For our music rehearsals, Dominic Muldowney handed out music sheets to each of us, and we gathered round the piano to practise, often accompanied by Robert Lockhart, the musical director.

Because the rehearsals were strenuous, any chance to nip away for tea or coffee and biscuits was always welcome. A member of the stage management team saw to it that fresh coffee, tea bags and hot water were always available. In the theatre you are trusted to put money in the tin can left next to the urn for contributions.

As the weeks went by I lost a stone and a half in weight, and my muscles became more alert. David's persistence, gentle in tone at first, but forthright and tough in the later stages, forced us to become more and more agile as the production gained momentum.

The Piper and Toffee in full rehearsal, showing their microphones (see p47)

The final part of the 'call' for each day was the wig and costume appointments, which had to be arranged around rehearsals. With some of us steadily losing weight, the wardrobe supervisor was always having to make final adjustments!

The children's costumes

One of the most enjoyable parts of the experience for the children was assembling their costumes.

As rats they wore black tights and black tops, which they provided themselves. To these were added the rat tails, which they made, and the famous masks.

The cardboard rat masks were provided by the theatre, but were cut out, folded and individually painted with luminous paint by the children. They

The basic rat costume, in sinister black

A fine example of the rat masks

looked very spooky on stage. Some rat masks were also on sale to the audience at the foyer bookstall, along with tapes of the songs from the show, copies of the script and other souvenirs.

When the children turned into the young inhabitants of Hamelin, they put on their costumes of cloaks. These cloaks were dark on one side, when they acted the school children from Lady Lucy Saveloy's Remarkable Academy for Children of Respectable Folk, and then turned dramatically to reveal a multi-coloured reverse side for the magical journey in the second half of the show.

The cloaks are brought on for the second half of the show

Half the fun for the children was making their costumes beforehand. The cloaks were all made in a school in Hammersmith, and their colours were one of the most memorable parts of the show.

The coloured side of the cloaks, en masse

Actors' costumes and make-up

Our costumes were designed with superb imagination by Sally Gardner. The coat of the toy stall owner, Arianalla Skiller, had toys sewn all over it. And the Rampant Umbrage's amazing monster form was still quite comfortable for Brian Hibbard to wear.

The toy stall owner's costume

Rampant Umbrage costume (left), Cosima Beamer (right)

Make-up was also designed by the costume designer, so that the appearance of each character was totally in keeping. But it is usually applied by the actor in person, as we are all perfectly experienced at doing our own make-up.

The Lady Mayoress applying her make-up

We did find, though, that the children were shocked by how exaggerated our make-up appeared when they saw us close-up. One young girl said to the Lady Mayoress, Patsy Rowlands, 'Do you mind if I say something? I think you're wearing a little too much make-up...'

The final part of our appearance was wigs, and these were made very expertly for each character who needed one.

Tidying up ('dressing') the wigs

Joint rehearsal

Each new group of children in the show had two days' rehearsal on the stage before their first performance.

Day one

To a carefully planned schedule, the 50 or so children were escorted into seats at the front of the auditorium, close to the stage. 'Front of house ushers' were always at hand to guide both them and their teachers from the Stage Door, along the endless corridors of the building and into position.

Then, under the guidance of Sarah Ream, the staff director, the children rehearsed on the set for the first time, without the principal actors present. This was when they learned to make their entrances and exits from the stage, where to wait in the wings, and how to co-ordinate movements on the stage.

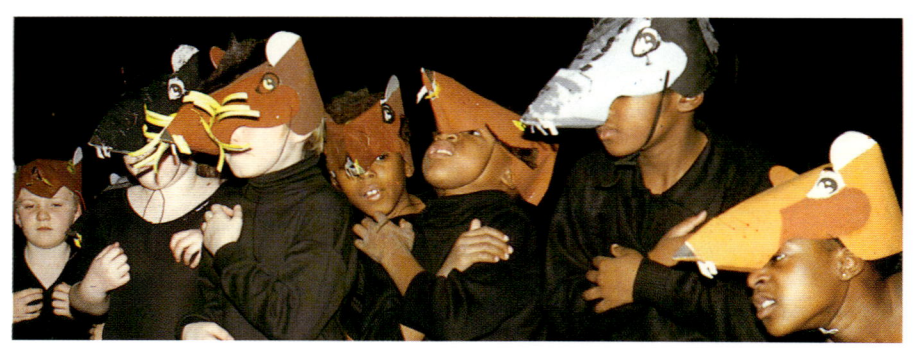

The rats, deeply involved in rehearsal

They rehearsed all their action in the show, which included singing the opening chorus, turning into rats to sing the grand 'Gorgonzola Moon', and finally drowning (happily for Hamelin) in the river.

The 'river' was in front of the first row of stalls seats, and the rats had to jump off the stage and crawl away right or left to the side exits – avoiding having their tails tugged by the young audience seated on the front row!

Later, as down-trodden pupils of Lady Saveloy's School, they practised singing their 'School Song' in long gowns. They also danced and sang the chorus of 'Rusty Robot', taking the side of the Piper against the Mayor. Sonia Friedman, from stage management, sang in place of Diane as Toffee Jenkins during rehearsal. They ended with 'Patchwork Rap', during which they reversed their dull cloaks to reveal the brightly-coloured side.

One key moment which needed 'placing' was the children's run up the side aisles of the theatre, out of the auditorium and back down the centre aisle to the stage.

Rehearsing around the fireside

As part of the journey sequence they also had to cross over a high bridge from which it was fatal to look down; act out being scared by a monster; find their way through the 'bottomless swamp' and demonstrate first feeling cold, then warming up by the fire, in the Freezing Forest of Forafter.

There were songs in between: joining in the Piper's song, 'Secret Country' where...

> *There are no prisons*
> *There are no poor*
> *There are no weapons*
> *There is no war...*

... and then dancing and singing inside the mountain, before the children had to get on and off the stage for the group curtain call and the end of the show.

All this made a very full and demanding first day's work.

Day two – afternoon

We now joined the children, starting by just chatting to everyone to break the ice. Then with full music, lights and all stage effects, the children repeated their contribution to the show along with us. At last they began to get a real idea of what the show would be like in performance.

Rigging the lights

The children soon lost their shyness during this joint rehearsal, and we also became better at gaining the trust of the new groups and, if necessary, toning down their *over* self-confidence!

Technical rehearsal

The 'tech.' is a long, tiring and sometimes even boring experience. It requires great patience from all involved. The tech. takes place two days before the first full performance in front of an audience. It is a special rehearsal for the technical staff, when the actors are there purely to help them practise their technical effects.

The director runs slowly through the technical requirements of the production. Sound, music and light cues have to be decided and entered on a special console. All the people from stage management, sound, lighting and the stage staff technicians have to learn to work in complete harmony, with perfect communication. Lights have to be rigged, adjusted and cued. All the stage effects have to be balanced correctly, and the actors made aware of any potential difficulties of working on this set.

Matthew Lynch at the technical rehearsal, cueing into the main consol

Entrances and exits have to be timed to music and light cues. Actors have to adapt to the acoustics of the theatre – they have to be heard clearly in this larger space, having got used to the smaller, easier space of the rehearsal room.

Props have to be placed. Quick costume changes have to be rehearsed. These technical details are all vitally important, because if cues were missed or props not there at the right moment, you would certainly notice it in the audience.

The sound technician, Paul Arditti

Dress rehearsal
From two days to go we move to one day to go, and the dress rehearsal. The school which was to be in the first performance was Dog Kennel Hill School, so they shared our dress rehearsal. Even at this late stage, in full costume, details still had to be attended to, and endless tiny improvements suggested. Finally, we moved on to the public preview performances, when the public can first come and watch, and Press Night, when the newspaper critics come to write up their reviews.

First night

Sonia Friedman, assistant stage manager, waiting for the show to commence

It's an exhilarating moment when you first play to a proper audience. You really feel the response from children and adults and somehow this gives the performance more pace and energy.

The Pied Piper waiting to go on stage

The press reviews were favourable. The Pied Piper was described as a superb children's actor –

> '... likeable but grave, quaint yet
> reassuring, soft-voiced but driven by a spry and
> sinister energy!'
> 'The Independent'

The children's memories of the performance were vivid; Gary from Dog Kennel School said:
'I liked King Rat; like a rock star, cool. Acting cool and mean!'

Nadine from the same school said:
'I liked it when Egbert said "I don't feel seasick", when he was meant to say, "I don't feel homesick".'

The Headteacher of Deptford Park Primary School described it like this:
'One child alone on an otherwise deserted stage, dwarfed by the towering set, singing in a piping, slightly husky, slightly quavering voice. One thousand four hundred people in the audience. Hushed. Captivated by that child at that moment'.

During the interval, most of us rarely returned to our dressing rooms, but sat around in the corridor at the edge of the stage, sipping tea and swapping comments about that particular performance.

Polly was a brilliant show dog: always in the right place at the right time, and never upstaging anyone! In real life she belonged to the actress who played Lady Lucy Saveloy, accompanying her to the theatre by car. Polly was a great favourite with the audience as well. She managed to lick Toffee's cheek in the final moments of the show.

We actors became very attached to each group of children, and it was always sad when we had to say farewell to another group. But we always signed their programmes as a souvenir.

The actors in performance

We played so many performances of *The Pied Piper* that we soon settled into a routine. Some days we had to play the show three times – morning, afternoon and evening.

King Rat doing his warm-ups

So pre-show preparation was essential: working through the warm-up so that we were physically and mentally ready to perform. This was especially necessary for the morning shows. You certainly need to warm up before singing at 10.30 in the morning!

Morning coffee, already with make-up on

For a morning show I always arrived at the stage door at 8.45 a.m. I'd collect any mail from my pigeon hole, and go on down to my dressing room, number 008. Next I'd put on my 'slap' (slap is slang for make-up). Then at 9 a.m., still in my own clothes, I'd walk up the corridor to the Green Room, where we all gathered for early morning conversation, catching up with the gossip and consuming a few gallons of coffee between us!

At 9.15 a.m. we started the physical and vocal warm-up, with Robert on the piano. We sang some scales, and did some stretching exercises, to tone up the larynx and body muscles in preparation for performance. Then we practised a couple of numbers from the show, and sometimes, for some reason, a snatch of 'Somewhere Over the Rainbow'.

The assistant musical director, Paul Maguire, cajoling us into song practice

When I returned to my dressing room, my dresser helped me get into my padding and the costume. I'd be ready at last, no longer the slim figure from the exercise room, but a rotund and floury miller!

One last chore was to attach the radio microphone to the top of my apron, with the battery pack placed carefully in a side pocket. This was because our songs had to project right to the back of the theatre, against the sound of the full orchestra. Upstairs at 10 a.m. we tested the mikes on stage, to balance the sound levels with those of the band.

We were now ready to go and chat to the audience of children waiting in the foyer. We always did this in the role of our characters, so we had to be ready to answer sharp, enquiring questions from very young children.

Ten minutes before 'curtain up' it was time to go backstage and chat to our own children in the show, who had been through the same kind of warm-up. Then we waited in perfect silence while the red light glowed, forbidding noise backstage. But as soon as it switched to green we burst into our first entrance.

The children in performance

The children had a similar routine when we were doing performances.

The first point was that they were *never* late. Hetty from the theatre's Education Department made sure of that! One London coach firm was used to bus the children in from London schools and they were expert at planning a fail-safe route from each school.

Children arriving at the theatre

The children had to be in the theatre at least an hour before the first performance of the day. This gave them time to adjust to the idea of the performance, have a snack, and warm up their voices and bodies with similar exercises to our own. Then they climbed into their costumes, and were always ready for the show on time.

The front of house ushers

Getting into the rat masks

49

Four teachers and five front of house ushers used to lead the children to their entrance points in the wings and gather them up after every exit. Both teachers and ushers had to be dressed in 'blacks' so as not to be seen by the audience at the edge of the stage.

The children all enjoyed this routine as a break from their lessons, but they were probably learning more confidence and professionalism than they ever would have at school!

After the show

Two months after a school had participated in the show, the teachers were always invited back to an informal meeting to assess the benefits the children had experienced during their performances.

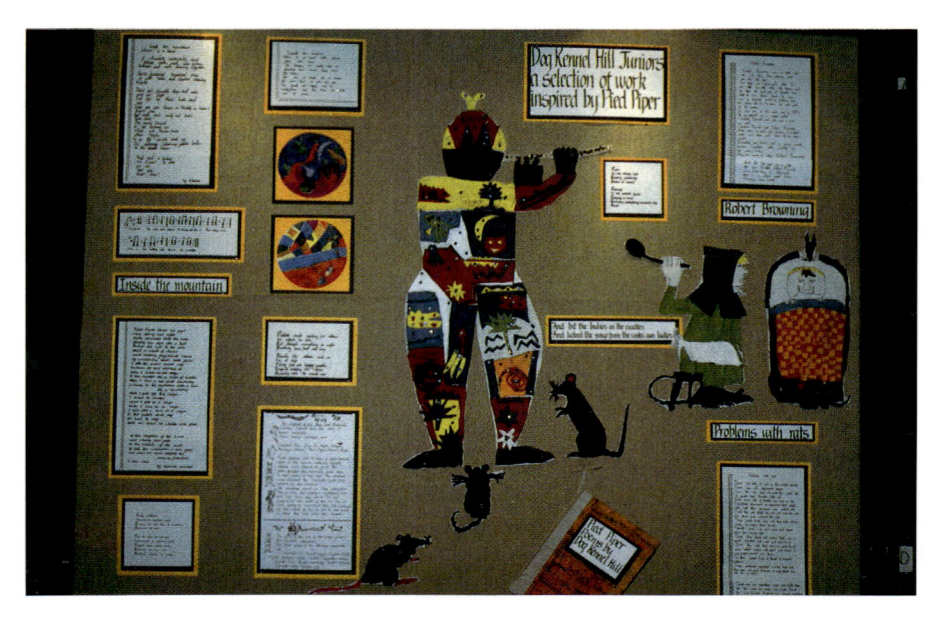

Work produced by children after the show

One teacher commented: 'When the performances commenced, the children would refer to the cast in conversation and in their writing work at school as Toffee, Piper, Mayor, Lady Lucy and King Rat. By the time they came to the end of the run they addressed them and wrote about them as Diane, Sylvester, Philip, Patsy and Brian. Despite being intensely involved with the characters and the story, the children made the transition many adults do not achieve, for they came to understand the distinction between the character and the actor's portrayal of that character.'

We also visited several of the schools after they'd finished their stint, and joined in tea while we sang again some of the numbers from the show and chatted happily about their days in *The Pied Piper*.

Sylvester comes back to see the schools again

The work of the children from Deptford Park School exhibited in the Theatre foyer along with the work of children from other schools

Perhaps the children themselves can best sum up what they felt about it all. These comments all come from work which schools produced after they'd finished in the show:

Deniz When we watched ourselves in the interview on TV it was really good, because it was us and not the boring old news.

Nadine I wanted to do the show for ever and ever.

Lisa When I first went on stage I felt stiff and excited. I closed my eyes and I was shaking. At the beginning of the song 'Hamelin Town' I had to look up at the ceiling when the song went 'from vermin was a pity'. I then had to shout 'RATS'. I came off the stage happy and excited.

Arnette On the stage, music playing, people cheering, actors singing, lights looking down on us. Nervous, a funny feeling inside. Big stage, everyone running around, rats' masks glowing. On stage, acting as though we were freezing, polystyrene snow falling on our hands. Running into the mountain, lights flashing. Smoke that smells like burning wood. It's come to the end of the play. Everyone skipping and bowing. Relief, skipping up the aisle. Back in the changing room, teachers saying well done!